P9-DGR-882

An Angel in My House

An Angel in My House

Tobias Palmer

Illustrated by Betty Eming

AVE MARIA PRESS • Notre Dame, Indiana 46556

ISBN 0-87793-103-8

LCCCN: 75-22990

©1975 by Joseph Nichols Publisher

©1975 by Ave Maria Press. All rights reserved

No part of this book may be reproduced or transmitted in any
form or by any means, electronic or mechanical, including
photocopying, recording, or by an information storage and
retrieval system, without permission from the Publisher.

Printed in the United States of America

Art by Betty Eming

For to his angels he has given
command about you,
that they guard you in all your ways.
Psalm 91

ALL MY LIFE, I have lived among angels. And so have you. Angels surround us and embrace us.

Angels are messengers of the Lord. They communicate to us the "divine news" and the "glad tidings."

Sometimes I get up in the morning, even before the break of day, and I go into the parlor and sit down in the old green chair by the window and I begin to think of the past and all the things I've lost and all my sorrows.

But suddenly, sitting there in the room with me, is an angel, scarcely visible in the morning shadows, and the angel says to me, "Nothing is lost. All is treasured in heaven. You are alive. Lift up your heart. I am with you. I bring you greetings from paradise."

AN ANGEL IS THE MESSENGER — and, also, the message itself. Even if an angel says nothing to us, if it simply flashes by, we have been *told something*. The very presence of an angel is a "communication." Even when an angel crosses our path in silence, God has said to us, "I am here. I am present in your life."

WHEN I WAS VERY YOUNG, in the poverty of my childhood, I was awakened in the middle of an April night by the singing of the night-birds. And when I woke up I saw a youth, slightly older than myself, standing in the darkness at the foot of my bed. The youth was smiling upon me, tenderly and lovingly, and I whispered, "Who are you? What are you doing here?"

And the youth said, softly, like music, "I am your brother."

"But I don't have a brother," I told him. "I have two sisters and a mother and a father, but I don't have a brother. You've made a mistake!"

But the youth repeated, "I am your brother."

And as the night-birds sang outside the window and the honeysuckle flowered, sweetly, on the vine, a great joy came over me as though some kinsman I had forgotten was now revealed to me, as though some relationship of which I was completely ignorant was now made known to me.

"I am your brother," the youth said, "and I am an angel of the Lord."

And as I experienced the happiness of that April night, I knew my life had turned into its proper direction.

I have encountered many angels in my lifetime, in my travels. Have seen them frolicking far away on the hillside in southern Ireland. Have heard them singing from the tops of cathedral spires in old Quebec. Have seen them brooding—like violet clouds—in the Parisian twilight over Notre Dame. Have seen them flash like golden birds through the intense heat of August as I tromped my way through the ruins of ancient Crete. Have seen them skim across the water off the coast of Spain. Have heard their footsteps, just behind me, in the aisles of St. Paul's and have heard their wings, rustling just above me, in the cloisters of New York.

ANGELS ARE INVISIBLE, but they can be seen —when the eyes of the spirit are open.

One does not often look upon an angel directly. More often one sees an angel *obliquely*. Out of the corner of one's eye. A fleeting glimpse. A suspicion. A "maybe and perhaps." A "feeling" one has.

When we look up from our busyness and ask, "Is there someone here? Is there an angel lurking in the room?" then, indeed, we are experiencing the presence of an angel. In our own suspicion is the truth. Our very question is an answer. We would never have looked up in the first place if an angel had not touched us—lightly—and stirred our senses into a divine awareness.

Angels appear as Light. As Form. As Motion.
Angels appear as the sound of distant music, as the
faint perfume of distant flowers.

Angels make use of our dreams. They give surprise
performances in the theaters of our sleep. In the
costumes of happiness, they play their parts in
divine comedies. And play their parts in dramas of
self-effacing love; the discovery of one's *true* self;
the reformation of the inner being.

ONE EVENING I invited my friend George over to watch television. When I heard someone at the door at eight o'clock I assumed it was George and I went to let him in. When I opened the door, there stood an angel.

"Why are you dressed up like an angel, George?" I asked.

"My name isn't George," the angel said. "I'm a messenger of the Lord."

"Where's George?"

"George is safe. He'll be along in a minute. He's running late."

"And what can I do for you?" I asked. "If you're an angel—"

The angel laughed. "I'm an angel indeed and I bring you good news! I bring you the news that your faith will rise again, that you will be able to face the world again tomorrow, that you will have strength to do the work that must be done, that you will be given opportunities to bring compassion and mercy into the lives of others, that your eyes will be opened to beautiful things and beautiful experiences and beautiful people in this world, and that God is forever present in your life and in the life of all mankind."

Then the angel laughed again with joy—and disappeared. And when George arrived, we didn't watch television, but we took a walk around the block, beneath the maples and the summer stars, and I listened to George tell about his troubles, about his poor health, about his business failures. And I did my best to comfort him. To share with him my hope and expectations. To give him the love of my friendship. To walk with him as far as I could. To open his eyes. And to show him the angel who, even then, was walking beside us and listening to all that we said.

ANGELS HAVE THEIR WORK TO DO. Not only are they messengers, but they are guardians as well.

They guard the gates of innocence and righteousness.

They guard the sleeping children.

They guard old men and women rocking in their chairs.

They guard us in the raging storm.

Angels also "lift and carry"—transporting us when we cannot transport ourselves.

They help us move from one room to another, from the old room of our mistakes into the new room of a better life.

They help us lift the heavy weights that block our way.

They help us climb over the stone walls that separate us from our fellowman.

They lift us up.

They lift up our souls and give us wings.

And angels guide us through seasons and celebrations.

I hear their trumpet calls on the first day of a new year.

I watch them unfold the green leaves of spring.

I hear their trumpet calls on Easter morn.

I watch them raise the summer grass and the summer flowers.

I watch them harvest grapes and apples and pears beneath the autumn skies.

I watch them gather birds with broken wings from the fields of winter snow.

I hear the trumpet calls of Christmas night.

As I make my way across the calendars of life, I
hear the angelic drums and tambourines.

Angels dance. Stately. In simple patterns. Around.
And back again. In perfect form. I have seen them
dance, their hands folded in front of them, their
hands lifted high, their steps in a strong and
glorious rhythm, dancing forth into the west, the
north, the east, the south, *knowing where the
center is, knowing how the circle turns, knowing
how to measure out their portions of beauty, love
and adoration.*

I have seen angels dance in a ring, holding hands,
laughing, making the beatific rose, making the
mandala of light and ecstasy.

I have known angels to dance through me, to dance
through my arms and legs, to lift me up into their
celebration, to set my hands a-clapping in the
middle of the day, to set me whirling in both
public and private places.

ONCE UPON A TIME, three sisters—all rosy-cheeked middle-aged Irish ladies—ran a boarding house in Columbus, Ohio. When their boarding house was full, they had—each day —fourteen roomers sitting down for breakfast and dinner. The fourteen roomers and three sisters took their meals at a huge, long table around which were placed eighteen chairs, and upon which were placed eighteen plates.

Inevitably, a roomer would ask one of the sisters, "Why is there an extra place, Miss Rose? You expecting somebody else?"

And Miss Rose or Miss Martha or Miss Florence would always answer, "You never know. An angel might drop in."

"An angel?" the roomer would ask incredulously.

"Even if he wasn't hungry, we'd want to offer him

something. To be polite. We'd want him to sit with us."

"Well, my goodness," the roomer would say. "You ever had such a visitor? You ever had an angel show up?"

And Miss Rose and Miss Martha and Miss Florence would smile knowingly at one another, remembering a wonderful day from years ago when an angel had surprised them right at dinner time and had taken his place at the dinner table and had given his blessing to the sisters and their food and all their boarders. Ever since that miraculous day, the sisters had been waiting for the angel to come back again—and they always put out the plate for him, and the white linen napkin, and the silverware, and the crystal goblet.

YOU LIVE AMONG MANY PEOPLE.

Save a place for an angel.

You live and work in the crowd.

Hold up a candle in the dark to let the angel see that you are thinking of him and making room for him within the multitude of humanity.

Even if you live alone, try to have two chairs. *An angel may visit you.* If you can afford only one chair, rise and leave it empty if an angel comes to see you. It is only good manners that you should stand and the angel sit down. If you are so poor you have no chairs at all, then you and the angel will both have to stand, but you should say to the angel, "Lean on me and rest." And if the angel rests against you, then you will no longer care about chairs or houses or wealth or poverty or loneliness, but you will be blessed and full of joy and not be weary.

I T IS EASY TO BE SENTIMENTAL about angels—but angels are something more than "sugar and spice" and "white chiffon dresses" and "golden harps" and "feathery wings." Angels can be very strong and tough, and in their service to us, they often challenge us and confound us and startle us and even knock us about, wrestling with us—as one of them did with Jacob—through the night. They struggle with us in order that we may be challenged into new awareness, new identity, new perspective. They pound upon our lives when our lives have gone to sleep. They waken us from apathy and sterility and dull comfort. They blast us out of fantasies into realities.

In some of the artistic depictions of angels, we see them carrying swords and spears. These are the weapons of reformation and transfiguration. Angels do not bring violence or militancy, but they do bring us the event of "death and transfiguration," wherein the old man is wounded and dies and the new man is born and resurrected. When an angel slashes through us with the golden blade, we are indeed undone and devastated. When an angel drives the weapon home, we are purged of all our fraud and pretense, and the True Man within us is released, rescued by the angelic raid upon the prison of our secularism and naturalism.

Angels comfort us by keeping us alive. By keeping us on our toes. Quiet and gentle as they usually are, the angels are not ever passive. They are always in action—even in the still, motionless action of standing and abiding with us.

MY COUSIN, WEBSTER, has a collection of angel figurines. He's collected some forty or fifty over the years, thanks to the gift-giving of his sister, Louise, and of others who love him and remember him at Christmas time. He displays the figurines on a set of shelves that he calls "Little Heaven."

I always enjoy examining the figurines—seeing the smoky pewter one that came from Mexico and the bright-green porcelain one from Ireland and the hard, brown, wooden one from Germany. The figurines come in a wonderful array of materials and shapes—plastic, glass, cornhusk, velvet; kneeling, standing, embracing, singing, playing musical instruments. Some make *real* music— china figurines turning to music-box carols.

I enjoy the figurines—realizing how artists and craftsmen struggle to depict the angelic form and the angelic face.

Realizing how man has always struggled to picture to himself the "presence" that he has always known and experienced—within, around, and about himself.

Realizing how man has always struggled—the struggle being a rich and wonderful part of his life —to express in art, in music, in words his "knowledge" of the angels, his knowledge of their transcendent reality.

Just as I struggle now in these words to say the ineffable truth about the angels and to share these reflections and ruminations with you.

DO NOT TRY TO BE "logical" about angels. Do not try to cage the angels in reasonable categories. Angels exceed all logic and they are more magnificent than our reason can comprehend.

Do not count the angels. The census of the angels is God's affair—not man's. One angel is enough to transform our lives. The existence of one angel is enough to overwhelm us with glory and to confound our secular-mindedness. How many angels are there? Enough. God's plenty. One? A billion? Whatever God deems to be sufficient in our lives, such a number there will be. And always has been.

TRADITIONALLY, there exists a hierarchy of angels—the nine orders—from "angel" to "seraphim." But these nine orders are actually the degrees of spiritual intensity that any angel can achieve. That is: as an angel "flowers" and "brightens" in the intensity of his own angelness, so he seems to achieve a "higher order." This angelic intensity can lift an angel to seraphic heights.

(Just as we ourselves can be in grace—but at certain times our grace flames into ecstasy; at other times, it is something quiet and still.)

An angel—sometimes—prefers to be only an "angel"; at other times he "lets go" into the fiery passion of glory and he climbs the ladder of increasing splendor.

The traditional hierarchy of angels is not a hierarchy of authority or power, but a spectrum of vibrancy —from cool humility at one end to blazing assertion at the other—a spectrum of possibilities through which the angels range according to the needs placed upon them, according to the demands of the particular situation, according to the requests of God and the petitions of frail human beings.

Angels enter our lives at the invitation of our spirit.

Angels penetrate our being. They penetrate our minds, our thoughts; the network of our nerves; the dark cells of our blood; the caverns of our psyches. We feel their presence in the tips of our fingers, in our own gestures of gentleness, in the gracious turn of our bodies. Angels penetrate our being—flooding and charging us with grace.

Oh angel! I am an empty house! Inhabit me! Move in! Make me your dwelling place!

SEXLESS THEMSELVES, angels do not like to be confined within our sexuality. When they penetrate our being, they dispense with our sexuality and while we are angelically occupied, we forget our "maleness" or our "femaleness" and know ourselves only as persons and look upon all others as persons. Our eyes see beyond the confines of gender.

Angels do not marry. They do not "make love." Yet they love and express love.

Their love is "beyond the body." They participate in a communion of like-mindedness and in a communion of common awareness of beauty and in a communion that comes by standing together in the Light of God.

To express love, angels do not look at **one another**, but look at something beyond themselves.

Let us imitate the angels, you and I. Let us love one another by loving that which is beyond and above us. Let us express our love by sharing in the common task or by looking upon the beauty that is distinct and separated from us. Let us turn our attention to the landscape, the music, the sunset, the painting. Let us turn our attention to the child who needs us. Let us know one another indirectly as our attention meets "out there" in common achievement and common experience.

Q

UESTIONS AND ANSWERS about the angels:

Q.   Do angels have a sense of humor?

A.   *Yes. A gentle humor. A humor meant to delight us and perhaps even to perplex us. Angels will sometimes place an extra star in heaven when some astronomer is looking through the telescope. Or they will turn the moon around. Sometimes the angels will make five-leaf clovers. Or hide the silver thimble. Or toss our lady's hair with a sudden breeze.*

Q.   What do angels eat?

A.   *They don't. They have no need for human food. Yet sometimes, when temporarily in human form, they may drink some water and eat a small piece of plain bread—to be sociable.*

Q.   What do angels wear?

A.   *Being incorporeal, they wear nothing—save when they appear in human form to human beings. Then they wear whatever is appropriate. Their most popular costume is a long white gown, tied at the waist, since that's what most human beings expect them to wear. Sometimes, though, if necessary, they will wear a business suit or a house dress or a fireman's uniform.*

Q.   Do angels attend church?

A.   *Yes, if it's a real church.*

Q.   How large are angels?

A.   *Large enough. They make themselves any size they want. For little people, they are little. For big people, they are big. Their average height— in human form—is five feet ten inches.*

Q.   How should one address an angel?

A.   *In the old days one always tried to address an angel by some specific name—such as "Gabriel" or "Michael" or "Israfel." But nowadays the* preferred form of address is simply "angel." Angels make very little of personal identity, emphasizing rather their "interchange" with one another and emphasizing their involvement in the total task of God's work.

Speaking to one angel, you speak to all. Calling upon one angel, you call upon the multitude of angels. If an angel is performing some particular task, you may call him by that task—such as "Angel of Mercy" or "Angel of Inspiration" or "Angel Who Walks With Me Through Darkness." But you need not worry about the angel's particular and individual name.

Q. How many angels can stand on the head of a pin?

A. This has been one of the most popular questions about angels over the centuries. The answer is that one angel and one angel only can stand on the head of a pin. If one angel is on the head of the pin and another angel comes along, then the two angels "merge" and become one angel again. This is one of the favorite games that angels play and as many as a thousand or ten thousand angels can "unite" upon the head of the pin. The inter-

*esting thing is that, as the number of angels in-
creases within the form of a single angel, so in-
creases the intensity of that angel's beauty. Indeed,
one of the most beautiful sights in the world is to
see—upon the head of a pin—a hundred thousand
angels "united" into a single, dazzling, penetrating
flash of light.*

MY FRIEND, ELIZABETH—now dead—gave me, shortly before she died, a list of the angels she had met during her 80 years upon this planet. She met most of her angels in the garden at the back of her house where she grew her flowers.

Angel of the Crimson Wings

Angel of the Flakes of Snow

Angel of the Plum Tree

Angel of the Purple Iris

Angel of the Eyes as Blue as Violets

Angel of the Robin Song

Angel of the Alabaster Hands

Angel of the Hands as Brown as Earth

Angel of the Hoe

Angel of the Summer Rain

Angel of the Autumn Wind

Angel of the Perfume of Lilacs in the Fading of the Day

YOU AND I may never meet, yet we are brought together by the angels themselves.

And though there are the deserts of space and the floods of time between us, we shall never be separated. An angel holds my hand, and your hand. We dwell that close together. Only an angel apart.

WHEREVER WE GO, the angels travel with us.

I go to the cemetery where my loved ones are buried. The winter snow has covered the land. The sycamore has been stripped of its leaves. Huddled in my winter coat, I stand and pray above their eternal sleep. And I am at peace. *There is an angel who guards the graves of those we love.*

I get off the bus in a strange city late at night. The streets are empty. The buildings are dark. I must try to find a room at a cheap hotel. I carry my suitcase through the desolation and the emptiness and the loneliness, under the melancholy street lights, through shadows. But I am at peace. *There is an angel who shares my wilderness, who stands in the deserted corner, who walks through the frightening city with me.*

The weather's hot. I'm worried about my job. I can't sleep. I bring all my troubles home from the office. I get out of bed and walk through the dark rooms. I go to the kitchen and get a drink of water. I go out on the porch and sit in the rattan chair. I try to be quiet so I won't wake up my family. I take a deep breath.

There is an angel who sits with me through the sleepless night, who shares the solitude and the discovery I begin to make about who I am and what really matters in my life. We talk about eternal things.

I am at peace.

GOD HAS PREPARED US with our imagination and our creativity in order that we may know the angels and benefit from them.

Once, when I was very ill, I woke up in a delirium, in the headiness of a high fever, and I reached over and took my wife's hand. She was sitting beside my bed, and I asked her, "Who is that other person in the room? Who is that person in the corner in the shadows? Who has come to visit me?"

The Angel of Death arrives when Mercy commands and calls. And the Angel of Death brings the message that God is present in our dying.

As our vision fails, this Angel fills our vision.

As we lose sight of this world, this Angel is "seen."

As our eyes darken, this Angel makes a miraculous light.

This Angel fills up our sight—and, whereas, in our living, we had seen the "things of this world," now, in our death, we see this stupendous angelic witness to the Glory of God.

Oh, Angel, be with me in my mortality, in the failing of my body, in my darkening hours. Be with me in the closing of this house. Be with me in the drawing of the dark blinds. Be with me in the termination of all that I have been. Be with me in this severing and this undoing.

I VISIT THE MENTAL HOSPITAL with my friend, the parish priest, and we walk through the wards where the young men are staring through the dusty windows at dusty sparrows far beyond in the dusty sky. One young man is weaving the sunbeams with his long, white, nervous hands. One young man is playing patty-cake into the empty air.

Oh, such a sad world. Such sorrow and grief! I pray that all this grief shall pass away! I pray that these young men will rise someday in glory from the gray confusion, from the labyrinth of their thoughts.

But even here—in the hospital, in the prison, in the asylum, in the dark places—the angels appear. *The angels are bearing gifts to the broken minds and the broken bodies and the broken lives. The angels are bearing grace and light and surcease. They are combing the tangled hair. They are holding the nervous hands. They are washing the distorted face.*

W E WERE HAVING A WONDERFUL PARTY, and all the children were home, and we were celebrating John's birthday, and Mother had baked a special white cake and we were looking at all the photographs we'd taken on the summer vacation up in Maine. Then we suddenly all stopped and grew very quiet and Mother said she thought she heard something out on the back porch and she thought maybe somebody was out there, trying to get into our house, and I said I'd go out on the porch to see if there was anybody there.

So I went through the kitchen and out on the back porch and I saw that the screen door was unlocked and I opened it and stuck my head outside and called into the twilight, "Is there anybody here? Is somebody wanting into our house? You're welcome to the party! Come on in! It's John's birthday!"

(Then I began to see the angels. They were every-where! They were entering the house with treasures in their hands—the treasures of Compassion and Understanding and Charity and Kindness and Endurance and Thoughtfulness and Faith and Peacefulness—treasures for John that he could use in his continuing growth, in the building of his life, in his continuing realization of beauty and joy.)

Then I went on back into the house and into the bright parlor and John was starting to open his gifts and Mother asked, "Well, was there anybody out there trying to get in?"

I laughed. "Oh, yes. It was a whole bunch of angels! I felt them rush by me into the house! They've come to celebrate!" And I took her into my arms and gave her a kiss. And I kissed John, too. And all the children.

I BELIEVE IN THE ANGELS—in their mysteries and miracles. In the messages they bear. In their loving presence.

And when I die, may angels lift me from this flesh.

May they share with me the viaticum of glory.

May they carry me into the new dimension of their eternal life.

And introduce me to the apostles and the saints.

And usher me—who was dead and reborn—into the sanctuary of God's eternal love.

YES: THERE ARE ANGELS IN HEAVEN. And yes: there are angels, here and now, upon this earth.

They demonstrate God's presence in the world and his ways of revelation—both his promise of heaven and his immediate love for you and me.

Angels are the bodying forth of God as he speaks to us, here and now, through the epiphanies of our daily lives—in the sunrise and the sunset, in the spring rain and the winter snow, in the planting and the harvest.

God speaks—and an angel steps forth to sing the joyous amen.

And is it possible that God may allow us (undeserving as we are) to serve with his angels in this world? To help in the communication of his glory and grace?

We sometimes say to the person who has treated us with charity, has comforted us, has performed the difficult but helpful task: *You are an angel.*

Say to the person who keeps the vigil, who bears the pain: *You are an angel.*

Say to the doctor, the teacher, the helpmate, the plumber, the clerk in the store, the parent, the child: *You are an angel.*

The gentle person—through his labors, his peacefulness, his goodwill, his generosity—may serve as a messenger for God, serve as an angel in our midst.

One April morning, I saw an angel watering his lawn and trimming the grass. I went over to the fence and said, "Looks like you're going to have some good roses this year," and the angel said, "Yes, I think so. They're coming along fine. That one bush there by the side of the house is going to bloom especially for you. I thought of you, and I planted it so you can see it from your window."

He was my neighbor.

One January afternoon, an angel walked ten blocks through the snow to take the lost child to its home. "You're the Peterson boy, aren't you?" the angel asked. "I know where you live. Up on Maple Street. You'd better hold my hand. Your folks will be wondering where you are." The angel laughed. "We should have worn our galoshes. The snow's getting deep." And after she left the child with his parents, the Petersons, the angel walked back the ten blocks to her own house, humming some remembered hymn in the face of the cold wind.

She was the widow who lived in the yellow bungalow across the way.

One August midday, I saw an angel putting shingles on the church roof. When it came noontime, he pulled a piece of bread from his tool box and ate the bread up there in the shade of the steeple. "You'd better come down," I called to him. "Take some time off. Have a good lunch."

He called back, "No. Want to get on with it. Want to finish up before it rains." Then the angel made a broad gesture out over the roof with his brown and weathered hands. "How does it look?"

"Fine," I said.

"Do you think so?" he called down. Then he smiled, almost shyly. "I want it to hold up for a long time. I'm trying to do good work. Turn out a good job."

He was my friend the carpenter.

Once I knew an angel to stay awake all night, sitting by the child while the child coughed and pulled at the cover, and the angel would reach over and put the wet cloth on the child's forehead, trying to bring down the fever, and the angel sat there till daybreak, not leaving the bedside for a single moment.

Once I knew an angel who gave up his white-collar job in Chicago and came back home to the farm to help his folks out, to help bring in the crops and pay the bills, and see that his younger brother, the one who had the talent, got his chance to leave the farm and go to college.

Once I saw a smiling angel in a wheelchair, rolling through the nursing home, pausing at this room and that room, asking, "Can I do anything for you today? Write some letters? Read to you? Do you want to visit?"

You are an angel, we sometimes say. *You can't fool me. I've found you out! I know an angel when I see one!*

I BELIEVE IN THE ANGELS. And in our capacity to move with the angels, bearing light and music, through this time and place.

Could you and I—like angels—learn to carry the good message?

Learn to lift the necessary burden?

Learn to comfort and console?

Learn to "be present" when and where there is human need?

And could we—like the angels—learn to acknowledge God in all that we are doing?

And reflect the angelic luminance of heaven—within ourselves and into the lives of others?